KIRSTY

THE KITTEN AND FRIENDS

BY J T SCOTT

KIRSTY

THE KITTEN AND FRIENDS
BY J T SCOTT

It was snowing in the garden.

Kirsty the Kitten was sitting by the window

watching the snow

fall from the sky.

It was nice and warm indoors,

but Kirsty was feeling sad.

The **Queen Bumblebee** flew down from her hive.

"Hello Kirsty," said the Queen Bumblebee.

"You look sad today. What's wrong?"

"I'm sad because I haven't seen my friend," said Kirsty.

"I think she has gone missing."

"Why don't you ask **Bumper the Bumblebee?**"

said the Queen Bumblebee.

"Perhaps he has seen your friend."

"Hello Bumper," said Kirsty.

"Have you seen my friend?

She lives next door.

The big black cat with four white paws."

"Hello Kirsty," said Bumper.

"I saw her on **Monday** by the trees.

Shall we see if she's still there?"

"It's not **Monday** any more," said Kirsty.

"I can see lots of pawprints in the ground by the trees,

but I can't see my friend."

"She must have moved on," said Bumper.

"Why don't you ask

Boris the Butterfly

perhaps he knows where your friend has gone?"

"Hello Boris," said Kirsty.

"Have you seen my friend?

She lives next door.

The big black cat with four white paws."

"Hello Kirsty," said Boris.

"I saw her on **Tuesday.** She was crossing the road.

Shall we see if she's still there?"

"It's not **Tuesday** any more," said Kirsty.

"I can see lots of cars,

but I can't see my friend."

"She must have moved on," said Boris.

"Why don't you ask

Chris the Caterpillar

perhaps he knows where your friend has gone?"

"Hello Chris," said Kirsty.

"Have you seen my friend?

She lives next door.

The big black cat with four white paws."

"Hello Kirsty," said Chris.

"I saw her on **Wednesday**.

She was trampling on my leaves.

Shall we see if she's still there?"

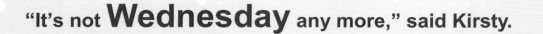

"It's not **Wednesday** any more," said Kirsty.

"I can see lots of broken leaves,

but I can't see my friend."

"She must have moved on," said Chris.

"Why don't you ask

William and Wendy the Worms

perhaps they know where your friend has gone?"

"Hello William, hello Wendy" said Kirsty.

"Have you seen my friend?

She lives next door.

The big black cat with four white paws."

"Hello Kirsty," said William.

"Hello Kirsty," said Wendy.

"We saw her on **Thursday**. She was squashing our tunnels.

William & Wendy's Home

Shall we see if she's still there?"

"It's not **Thursday** any more," said Kirsty.

"I can see the damage to your tunnels,

but I can't see my friend."

"She must have moved on," said William.

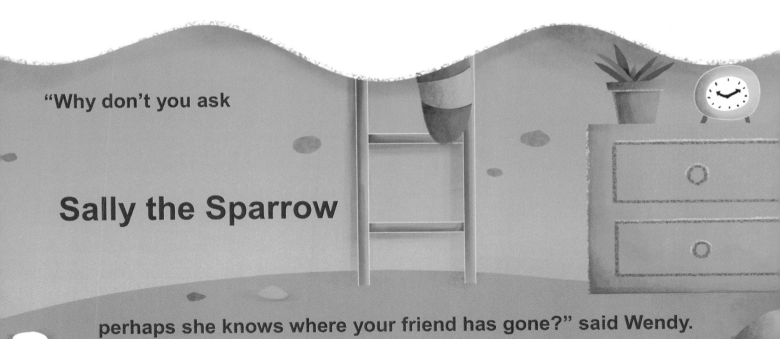

"Why don't you ask

Sally the Sparrow

perhaps she knows where your friend has gone?" said Wendy.

"Hello Sally," said Kirsty.

"Have you seen my friend?

She lives next door.

The big black cat with four white paws."

"Hello Kirsty," said Sally.

"I saw her on **Friday**.

She was looking for food in the bin.

Shall we see if she's still there?"

"It's not **Friday** any more," said Kirsty.

"I can see the bin is empty,

but I can't see my friend."

"She must have moved on," said Sally.

"Why don't you ask

The Three Fish

perhaps they know where your friend has gone?"

"Hello fish" said Kirsty.

"Have you seen my friend?

She lives next door.

The big black cat with four white paws."

"Hello Kirsty," said one of the fish.

"We saw her on **Saturday**. She stopped here for a drink.

But now our pond has frozen solid with ice,

so we can't swim to help you look for her."

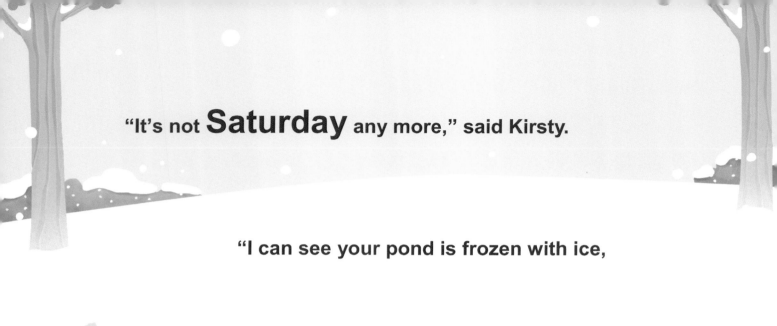

"It's not **Saturday** any more," said Kirsty.

"I can see your pond is frozen with ice,

but I can't see my friend."

"She must have moved on," said the fish.

"Why don't you ask

Gertrude the Gnome

perhaps she knows where your friend has gone?"

"Hello Gertrude" said Kirsty.

"Have you seen my friend?

She lives next door.

The big black cat with four white paws."

"Bumper said he saw her on **Monday**.

Boris said he saw her on **Tuesday**.

Chris said he saw her on **Wednesday**.

William and Wendy said they saw her on **Thursday**.

Sally said she saw her on **Friday**.

The Three Fish said they saw her on **Saturday**.

Today is **Sunday**. Please can you help me find my friend?"

Gertrude smiled and pointed at the barn.

"Today is **Sunday**," said Gertrude.

"There is another exciting week ahead.

Your friend is safe.

She is in the barn with her new litter of kittens."

"She will be pleased to see you and glad you have found her."

"Thank you everyone for your help this week," said Kirsty.

"My friend is safe and I have new kitten friends to play with."

KIRSTY
THE KITTEN AND FRIENDS
BY J T SCOTT

Kirsty the Kitten and Friends is dedicated to Mum & D2.

The moral right of J T Scott to be identified as the author
of this work has been asserted in accordance with the
Copyright, Designs and Patents Act 1988.

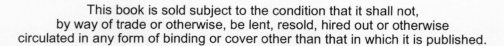

J T SCOTT

J T Scott lives in Cornwall surrounded by open countryside,
lots of castles, pens, paper and a vivid imagination.

She has also written the Sammy Rambles series
and created the inclusive game Dragonball Sport.

Sammy Rambles and the Floating Circus
Sammy Rambles and the Land of the Pharaohs
Sammy Rambles and the Angel of 'El Horidore
Sammy Rambles and the Fires of Karmandor
Sammy Rambles and the Knights of the Stone Cross

www.sammyrambles.com
www.dragonball.uk.com